Prairie
Animals

Prairie
Animals

1768

ENCYCLOPÆDIA BRITANNICA

CHICAGO •LONDON •TORONTO •GENEVA •SYDNEY •TOKYO •MANILA •SEOUL

Advisory Board

The Treasury of American Wildlife advisory board was established to help make this book series a unique effort toward further understanding of our wildlife resources. Members come from many walks of life and share a common interest in preserving America's priceless wildlife heritage.

Clifford L. Ganschow, advisory board chairman, has had an interest in wildlife and the outdoors from his days on an Illinois farm where he was born and raised. His undergraduate and graduate fields of study at Iowa State University were journalism and agricultural science. He has served in an editorial capacity on *National Wildlife* and *International Wildlife* magazines since their inception, and is chairman of a publishing organization that produces eight other outdoor and agricultural publications. In addition to his interest in conservation of natural resources, Mr. Ganschow has devoted considerable time to preservation of historic buildings and serves as a director of The Landmarks Preservation Council. He and his wife, Beverley, and their three school age children live in Woodstock, Illinois.

John L. Strohm, editor of *National Wildlife* and *International Wildlife* magazines, has traveled and observed the land and its wildlife in more than 90 countries around the world. He was the first correspondent to travel freely in Russia after World War II, with articles syndicated in more than 1,000 newspapers. In 1958 he became the first accredited American writer to penetrate the bamboo curtain to report on life in Red China and his written and film reports were shown throughout the nation. He is a journalism graduate of the University of Illinois, past president of the American Agricultural Editors Association and the author of three books. The Strohms raised a family of six children.

Dr. Lorin I. Nevling, Jr. is Assistant Director of Science and Education at the Field Museum of Natural History in Chicago. Dr. Nevling is in charge of the overall operations of the Museum's programmatic departments, including education and exhibitions. He was formerly Curator of the Gray Herbarium and Curator of the Arnold Arboretum at Harvard University, and also served as research assistant at the Missouri Botanical Garden. Dr. Nevling is a panelist member in the Museum Programs Section of the National Endowment for the Humanities and has served as consultant to the Biological Research Resources Program of the National Science Foundation. The Nevlings have five children.

Don McNeill's Breakfast Club made a "neighborhood of the nation" from 1933 to 1969 when it established a record as the longest lasting, continuous network radio program of all time. Millions of families still think of him as the man who came to their breakfast table and stayed on and on. After the Breakfast Club left the air, Mr. McNeill taught communications at Marquette University and Notre Dame. He has Honorary Doctorates from both these universities as well as Loyola and St. Bonaventure. The McNeills raised three sons and family summers are usually spent at a nature retreat near Chicago, where for 25 years they shared their lake and woods with underprivileged children.

Roger Tory Peterson is perhaps the best known wildlife illustrator in America, and is world renowned as an ornithologist, naturalist, author and lecturer. His *Field Guide to the Birds* has been called the most successful and influential bird book of all time. He was art director of the National Wildlife Federation for 30 years and presently is a consultant to the National Audubon Society. He has been the recipient of nine honorary doctorates and many medals and awards including the Gold Medal of the World Wildlife Fund. Dr. Peterson has traveled to remote corners of the world to observe and record wildlife. He lives in Old Lyme, Connecticut, and is married and has two children.

Dr. Kenneth Starr is Director of the Milwaukee Public Museum, which features outstanding displays of American Wildlife arranged in life-like dioramas. Over the years the Museum has become a field trip destination for Wisconsin families. He has worked with young people in several capacities, including principal of an American school in North China. Dr. Starr is an anthropologist with advanced degrees from Yale University, and was formerly associated with the Peabody Museum at Yale and with the Field Museum of Natural History in Chicago. Dr. Starr is current president of the American Association of Museums. The Starrs have two children.

Ray Arnett is an avid outdoorsman who has devoted much of his life to the preservation of wildlife. As a geologist, he roamed America's wild country seeking petroleum. Later he was appointed by Governor Ronald Regan to head the California Department of Fish and Game, where he served for eight years. He has served as a director of the National Wildlife Federation for 17 years, and two terms as president. He has been affiliated with many state and national conservation organizations. He has served as chairman of the Wildlife Conservation Fund of America and the Wildlife Legislative Fund of America. He lives in Stockton, California and has four children.

James Lockhart has specialized in wildlife art for more than 20 years. His realistic, detailed paintings have been featured in many books and periodicals in the outdoor field. A recent wildlife art calendar sold 1,300,000 copies and made him the recipient of his second national Mead Award of Merit. His paintings have been extensively reproduced on porcelain. Mr. Lockhart was graduated from the University of Arkansas and did graduate work at the Art Institute of Chicago and the American Academy of Art. He is an ardent conservationist and pioneered the issuance of a yearly print to raise funds for Ducks Unlimited. He lives in Lake Forest, Illinois, and has two children.

ISBN: 0-85229-368-2   © **1979 by Encyclopaedia Britannica, Inc.**   Printed in U.S.A.

Table of Contents

The Prairie

The center of North America was once covered by a huge grassland called the Prairie Belt.

This great sea of grass developed millions of years ago when the Rockies pushed up and blocked the flow of rain from the West. The prairie was very hot in summer and bitterly cold in winter. Most kinds of trees and bushes could not grow there. Only certain kinds of grasses and flowers survived.

These vast prairies attracted grazing mammals in enormous numbers. Had it not been for these animals, mostly buffalo and prairie dogs, trees and shrubs would have started to take over and the grasslands would have eventually become forest.

Before the arrival of the Europeans, humans had little effect on the prairies. The Plains Indians were hunters, not farmers.

But when the pioneers entered the prairies, the land began to change. Bison and prairie dogs were killed in vast numbers. Grasslands were plowed into farmlands.

Today, only remnants of the prairie are found in a few preserves. They show us how the center of our country once looked.

The eight animals in this book are well suited to the extremes of heat and cold and other conditions on the open prairie of central North America.

America's Prairie

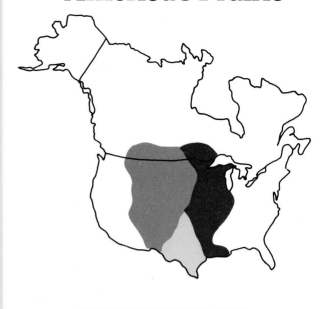

- ■ Grasslands
- ■ Oak-Savanna
- □ Mesquite-Grassland

Tall Grass

Pronghorn

This speedster survives in great numbers in the West. A strong sense of smell helps it spot danger. Pronghorns eat a wide variety of prairie plants.

Prairie Dog

Billions of prairie dogs once lived on the prairie. Only a few towns remain. They dig a tunnel for a home. Grass is their main food.

Jackrabbit

This hare is known for its long ears and fast, bounding pace. It's a favorite food of many predators. Jackrabbits eat grass, shrubs and bark.

Rolling Hills

Short Grass

Wooded Stream

Meadowlark

These sweet-singing birds love the shelter of tall grass. Nests are hidden on the ground. Larks eat insects, weeds, seeds and waste grain.

Bison

We call it "buffalo" but it actually is a bison. Over 100 million once grazed prairie grass. Man killed almost all of them.

Rattlesnake

This poisonous snake lives in grasslands and lower mountains. It rattles to scare enemies. Rattlesnakes eat small mammals and birds.

Coyote

The coyote has many enemies but still lives on the prairie. Rodents and rabbits are favorite foods. Ranchers consider the coyote a pest.

Prairie Chicken

Several species of this wary bird live in prairie states. You find them in brushy grasslands. They eat grass, seeds and insects.

The Pronghorn

If you have driven through the open grasslands of the West, you may have seen deerlike animals with large white rumps. These are pronghorns, the American antelope. When they run, their white rumps seem to flash. The white flashes are warnings to others of danger.

The pronghorn is not really a member of the antelope family. It is a native American animal and is found nowhere else in the world. Pronghorns have been on our western plains for millions of years. As the pioneers moved west, the pronghorns began to disappear. The grasslands they grazed on were plowed by farmers, and people hunted the pronghorns for their meat. In 1908, when there were only 20,000 pronghorns left, laws were passed to protect them. Their herds grew again. Today there are more than half a million pronghorns.

Pronghorns look a lot like deer. Their bodies are the same shape, but they are differently marked. Pronghorns are tan with two white stripes across the throat. They have a large white rump patch and white belly.

The rump hairs of a pronghorn are sparkling white and almost twice as long as the hair on the rest of the animal's body. When alarmed, the pronghorn raises each white rump hair to make it spread out. This motion almost doubles the size of the white patch. It catches the light of the sun, and the signal can be seen for several miles. When other pronghorns see the flash of white, they send the same signal on to the rest of the group. In a very short time, the entire herd is aware of danger.

Horns...or antlers?

Deer and elk have antlers. Each year, they fall off and new ones are grown. But horns never drop off. They are permanent. The pronghorn has horns that are different from those of any other animal in the world. It never loses them, but a hollow black sheath, or covering, on the horns does drop off each year. The sheath looks like fine black hair combed upward.

Both males, or bucks, and females, or does, have horns, but does' horns are very short. They are seldom more than three or four inches (eight or 10 centimeters) high. The horns of bucks are usually 12 to 15 inches (30 to 38 centimeters) high. The horns have two prongs, or points, thus, "pronghorn."

The private
life of the pronghorn

Pronghorns like to be with others of their kind. They sometimes travel in herds of 50 to 100.

The buck has a wide black stripe on his face from under his eyes to his nose. He also has a black patch on his neck. The doe does not have any black on her face and neck.

In the autumn, the breeding season begins. Each buck gathers several does together in a harem. The male works hard to keep his harem of does together. Sometimes a buck will try to take a doe from another buck's harem. When this happens, the two bucks may fight. They butt their horns together. The fight is over when one of the bucks turns and runs away.

In early winter, the breeding season is over. The bucks and their harems gather together again to form herds.

Alertness means survival

The flat, open areas where pronghorns live make it easy for them to be seen by their enemies. To survive, they have to sense danger from a distance so they can escape.

Pronghorns probably have the best eyesight of any American animal except the mountain sheep and mountain goat. With their large, bulging eyes, they can see backward and forward at the same time. It has often been said that pronghorns can see as well as people using binoculars.

Their sense of smell is their next most important warning system. If they cannot identify an object by sight, they may circle it to get its scent.

Pronghorns seldom settle down for long sleeps. Instead, they take little catnaps. They rest with their heads up. Pronghorns sleep for a short time, open their eyes for a quick look around, then sleep for a few more minutes. Even while they are sleeping, their noses are ready to catch the faintest scent of anything strange or dangerous. If a single pronghorn sees or smells something alarming, its white rump danger signal will send the entire herd galloping away.

Speedster of the prairie

The pronghorn is built for speed. It is the fastest animal in North America. The only faster animal in the world is the cheetah of India and Africa. The average running speed of a pronghorn is 40 to 50 miles (65 to 80 kilometers) per hour. Some have been recorded running 70 miles (110 kilometers) per hour for short distances.

The pronghorn will often race with horses or automobiles. Sometimes an entire herd will run next to a car. Then they put on a burst of speed and cross in front of it, as though showing they are faster than machines. When they have won the race, they stop and watch the car.

Pronghorns' legs look thin and delicate, but they are amazingly strong. Their power comes from their hind legs. Front legs help them keep their balance. When traveling at high speeds, pronghorns often move in long, graceful leaps. They can cover up to 27 feet (eight meters) in just one jump. The average distance is about 14 feet (four meters).

Their very large windpipes, large lungs and hearts also help pronghorns run. Though a pronghorn weighs about the same as a sheep, its heart is twice as large. These features allow the pronghorn to gulp great quantities of air while it is running. Getting more air into the lungs increases the pronghorn's endurance.

Kids will be kids

In spring, when the prairies are covered with blooming wild flowers, pronghorn mothers give birth to their young. The babies are called "kids" or "fawns." Pronghorn young are usually twins. However, the first time a pronghorn doe gives birth, she has only one fawn.

The little ones each weigh four to five pounds (1.8 to 2.3 kilograms) when they are born. They are covered with a beautiful, wavy, pale brown coat. They are not spotted, as are white-tailed deer fawns. Dur-ing their first days of life, the kids spend 20 to 22 hours a day resting and sleeping in the tall grasses that hide them. Each kid is hidden in a separate place. When their mother comes to them, they nurse for a short time, then drop down into the grass again until she returns. Newborn pronghorn kids have almost no scent. Because of this, a predator has a hard time finding them.

At the age of four days, pronghorn kids can run faster than a man. When they are

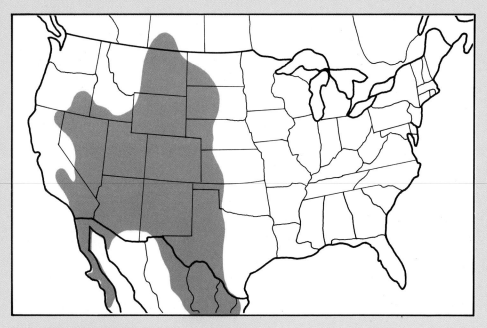

PRONGHORN FACTS

Habitat: Open prairies and sagebrush plains.

Habits: Nervous, curious. Active anytime, but mostly during the day.

Food: A browser. Eats weeds and grasses, sagebrush, saltbush, rabbitbrush, western juniper and bitterbush.

Size and Weight: A full-grown buck is 35-41 inches (89-104 centimeters) tall at the shoulder and four-five feet (1.2-1.5 meters) in total length. Weighs 100-140 pounds (45-65 kilograms); does weigh about 20 pounds (nine kilograms) less.

Life Span: Average is eight years, but can live up to 14.

Locomotion: Fastest land animal in North America, with speeds up to 70 miles (110 kilometers) per hour.

Voice: Kids have a high-pitched bleat, sometimes answered by a lower bleating from the doe. Both sexes snort when angered or alarmed.

between two and three weeks old, the youngsters join the herd with their mother. They play games as all children do. They chase each other, butt their heads together and jump into the air, kicking up their hind legs. Often, groups of kids will race at high speed in a big circle, then run back to their mothers.

Pronghorn mothers sometimes leave their kids with "babysitters." One mother may be left in charge of 10 to 12 youngsters while the other mothers wander off to feed, rest or just "get away from their kids."

The Prairie Dog

When cattle moved onto the prairie 100 years ago, what animal would you say was their biggest competitor for grasses? Buffalo? Pronghorn? No, it was a little three pound (1.4 kilogram) animal about a foot and a half (0.5 meter) long—the black-tailed prairie dog. Billions of them once lived in "towns" scattered over the length and breadth of shortgrass prairies.

Travelers crossing the plains during the settling of the West were charmed by the busy, busy scenes in prairie dog towns. The little squirrel-like mammals live in burrows 25 to 75 feet (eight to 23 meters) apart. One town in western Kansas stretched for 100 miles (160 kilometers). Another in Texas covered 25,000 square miles (64,750 square kilometers) and probably contained about 400 million prairie dogs. The total population in pioneer times was probably more than five billion.

When people began to use the plains grasses as food for cattle, the competition began. The prairie dogs in the Texas town, for instance, could eat as much grass as 1½ million cows. For ranchers, this would never do, and the old residents lost out to newcomers. All but a few colonies of prairie dogs were destroyed in extensive rodent-control programs. There are still a few places where you can see a prairie dog town and imagine what it must have been like before so many were destroyed by poisoning. They are located in Wind Cave National Park, Devils Tower National Monument and other preserves.

Home is where you dig it

The homes in a prairie dog town are underground. Each animal digs its own with the long sharp claws on its front feet. After loosening the soil, the prairie dog passes it under its body back to the hind feet and kicks it out. The dirt really flies. It is hard to believe this can be done in a tunnel that drops almost straight down from three to 16 feet (one to five meters) or more before turning horizontal. The opening is six to eight inches (15 to 20 centimeters) wide, and the tunnel narrows quickly to four or five inches (10 or 13 centimeters). Near the surface is a small side chamber for listening, watch-

ing and turning around after a dash to safety. Branching off the horizontal section at the bottom is a chamber about nine by 11 inches (23 by 30 centimeters), lined with grass. This is where the young are born and live.

The prairie dog builds an earth mound about four feet (1.2 meters) across and two feet (0.6 meters) high around the mouth of the burrow. It pushes and packs the earth firmly with its nose. The mound keeps the tunnel from flooding in times of heavy rainfall. A group of these mounds may be the first sign that you are in a prairie dog town. The animals work hard to keep their homes in good condition and the same family may live in a town eight years.

Keeping the population up

Prairie dogs mate in early spring, and the young (usually five) are born 35 to 37 days later. A newborn pup is blind, hairless and weighs about one-half ounce (14 grams). In about four weeks, it has fur. At five weeks its eyes open and it barks. At six weeks, it makes its first trip to the surface and eats its first grass. Before then its food has been milk from its mother.

By September the pups are weaned, and the mother leaves the burrow to find or dig another. Soon the pups leave one by one and move to nearby vacant burrows, where each lives alone. It's easy to see how the towns become large.

How a prairie dog survives

The prairies are dry and treeless, hot in summer, cold in winter. By eating in the morning and evening, the prairie dog avoids hot midday sun. Its eyes have orange-colored lenses, which filter glare from the sun. When there is rain, the animal will drink from puddles. But in dry weather it depends on its body to manufacture water from the food it eats.

By fall, these rodents are plump enough to hibernate. That is, their bodies have stored enough fat to let them pass the winter in a deep sleep with no food. Actually, prairie dogs do not hibernate. Some may sleep underground for days, but prairie dogs may also be seen out in winter, even on very cold days.

A cousin lives nearby

The black-tailed prairie dog has short legs and tail and a stout body. The pouches inside its cheeks, plus small ears and short, coarse, dense fur, give it a roly-poly look, complemented by rough-and-tumble behavior. Of course, it has a black tail.

The black-tailed's look-alike cousin is the white-tailed prairie dog. It has a slightly smaller, slightly paler body but dark face and—yes—a white tail. This rodent prefers open or somewhat brushy mountain valleys. It is less likely to live in colonies or towns and does not need to build a mound around its burrow to prevent flooding. Where winters are extremely cold, the animal hibernates from November to March.

times are food for both snakes and owls.

Danger is everywhere around a prairie dog town. Coyotes, ferrets, snakes, ravens, eagles and hawks all eat prairie dogs.

The social scene

Although a town may extend for miles, an individual prairie dog limits its travels to an area about 40 yards (37 meters) in diameter. The animals are alert, busy, playful and friendly. There may be from five to 35 individuals per acre (0.4 square kilometers). Cliques or clans, called coteries, within a town protect their territory against others.

When a group of prairie dogs are feeding or playing, one always stands guard to sound the alarm in case of danger. The prairie dog takes its name from the barking sound it makes. At the alarm, the dogs race in all directions to home tunnels. After checking for a false alarm, they are soon out in the sunshine again resting or feeding.

The myth

Because owls and snakes are often found in the burrows of a prairie dog town, people sometimes assume the animals are "friends." This idea is false. A burrowing owl may use a deserted prairie dog tunnel rather than dig a burrow of its own. A prairie dog is quick to fight an owl found in its own tunnel. A snake may hunt for food or escape the hot sun in a burrow. If it does, the prairie dog gets out. Young pups some-

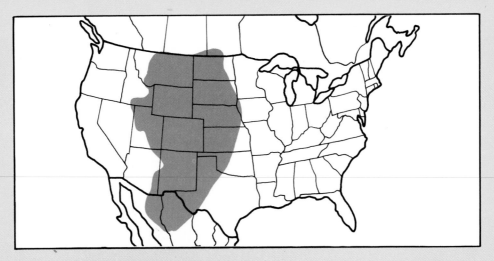

BLACK-TAILED PRAIRIE DOG FACTS

Habitat: Short-grass prairies; dry upland prairies.

Habits: Live in colonies. Very active during day, particularly morning and evening.

Food: Mostly grasses and herbs; some insects.

Size and weight: Total length 14-17 inches (35-42 centimeters), tail three-four inches (7½-10 centimeters); weight two-three pounds (0.9-1.4 kilograms).

Life Span: In captivity, 10-11 years.

Locomotion: Runs along ground on short legs.

Voice: Danger signal, two-syllable bark; also chittering, chattering and rasping noises.

The Jackrabbit

When early explorers first came upon this animal, they called it the jackass rabbit because its ears look like mule ears. In time the name shortened to jackrabbit. Black-tailed and white-tailed jackrabbits are most common, but there is also an antelope jackrabbit and possibly a fourth kind, or species, found only in southern New Mexico.

A jackrabbit, regardless of its name, is a hare. Like other baby hares, jackrabbits are born with full coats of soft fur. Their eyes are open, and they are strong enough to take a few steps. Newborn rabbits, on the other hand, are naked and blind.

The black-tailed jackrabbit is the most often seen. It lives in sparse deserts of the Southwest as well as on the open prairies. Like other hares, its coat has three layers: the short, thick, silky underfur; a layer of longer, coarser hairs; and a third layer of even longer hairs. The black-tailed is a little smaller than the white-tailed, but its ears are longer. Its head looks small for its big ears and big body. It is grayish-brown with black-tipped ears and a black streak on the top of its tail that can be seen even at a distance. But when it sits stock still in the shade of a low plant, one can hardly see the animal, let alone its tail.

The white-tailed jackrabbit is more northern and also lives in mountains as high as 12,000 feet (3,658 meters). In summer it is brownish-gray, like dry leaves, with a white tail and black ear tips. Winter brings snow where the white-tailed lives. The rabbit then sheds its brown coat and grows a white coat that blends with snow.

The jumping jack

Jackrabbits are the fastest animals on the prairies except for the pronghorn. The black-tailed can run 30 to 35 miles (50 to 55 kilometers) an hour. The white-tailed is even faster. It can lope along at 35 miles (55 kilometers) an hour or spurt up to 45 miles (70 kilometers) an hour. In one jump it can clear 17 feet (five meters). When cars first began to travel on prairie roads, drivers delighted in watching these big hares racing along beside them.

Jackrabbits have unusually long and strong hind legs and a very springy way of moving, almost like a bouncing rubber ball. The black-tailed usually has a shorter hop than the white-tailed. Every few jumps it leaps quite high, so that it can look for enemies in the brush.

Jackrabbit young

It's surprising how little information we seem to have about the early lives of jack-rabbits. They are very secretive with their young. Hares do not use burrows to raise their offspring. They prefer a simple hollow hidden under a bush or low branch or in grass.

The breeding season of the black-tailed jack extends from December until the next September, and several litters are raised each year. It takes an average of 43 days from the time the adults mate until the young are born. There may be from one to six babies in a litter, but usually two to four. Their first food is mother's milk.

Farther north, the breeding season for the white-tailed jackrabbit is shorter. There are fewer litters in a year, with three to six babies in a litter, usually four or five. It will be a year before any of these have young of their own.

A special digestive system

Black-tailed jackrabbits eat mostly grasses and herbs and also browse on shrubs and cactus. The jack has a special means of digesting this coarse food. Partly digested food is excreted as soft pellets and is quickly swallowed again. Tiny organisms in the hare's body further digest the pellets so that all the nutrients can be used. Biologists speculate young hares may get the microbes they need to digest plants by eating their mother's soft pellets.

Highs and lows of jackrabbits

Jackrabbit numbers go through a cycle of highs and lows. These changes in populations, particularly of the black-tailed jack, cause similar cycles in the predators that depend on the jacks for food—coyotes, eagles, foxes, bobcats and hawks, to name a few. A complete cycle requires about seven years from high to low to high. When working naturally, this see-sawing of numbers of predator and prey, along with other factors, controls the jackrabbit population.

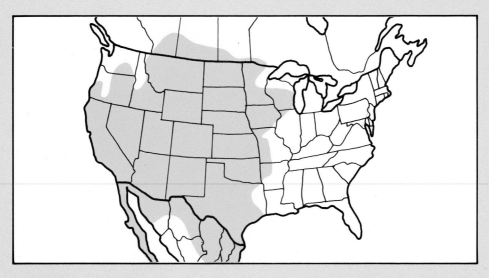

JACKRABBIT FACTS

Habitat: Black-tailed jackrabbit—open grasslands and arid terrain. White-tailed jackrabbit—open grasslands from the Great Plains to elevations of 12,000 feet (3,658 meters).

Habits: Active evening to early morning year-round. Solitary, for the most part.

Food: Grass, herbs, cactus, shrubs, bark.

Size and Weight: Black-tailed jackrabbit—length, head and body, 17-21 inches (0.4-0.5 meters), tail 3½-4 inches (0.1 meters), ear from notch six-seven inches (0.15-0.18 meters); weight, three-seven pounds (1.3-3 kilograms). White-tailed jackrabbit—length, head and body, 18-22 inches (0.46-0.56 meters), tail 3-4½ inches (0.13-0.15 meters), ear from notch, five-six inches (0.08-0.11 meters); weight, five-eight pounds (two-four kilograms).

Life Span: Most do not survive one year in the wild.

Locomotion: Bounding hops at 35-45 miles (55-70 kilometers) per hour.

Voice: Usually quiet, squeals when surprised or frightened.

But many of the jack's enemies were destroyed during the settling of the West. Jackrabbit populations skyrocketed. They competed with livestock for prairie plants and were very destructive to crops. Farmers and ranchers held jackrabbit roundups to get rid of these threats to their livelihood. Today there is only a small part of the population that once existed before the prairie was carved up.

The Meadowlark

There are two kinds of meadowlarks in our country, and neither actually is a lark. Both are members of the blackbird family and are related to orioles, bobolinks and redwings. One is the eastern meadowlark; the other is the western meadowlark. They look so much alike that it takes an expert birdwatcher to identify them where they are found together. Even their nests and eggs are much alike.

To be sure which is which you must hear the bird sing. Each kind of meadowlark has its own song. (Females do not sing.) The eastern meadowlark seems to say "spring o' the year" or "tee-you, tee-year." The song of the western meadowlark is a flute-like, gurgling melody of six to 10 notes, entirely different from its eastern relative.

But even if you hear a male singing, you can't always be sure if you're listening to an eastern or western meadowlark. In some places the two have learned each other's songs. The females of each species seem to know the difference, however. They apparently choose their mates by their distinctive call notes.

Most meadowlarks fly south for the winter, but some males stay behind and get the pick of good nesting territories the following spring. This helps attract females.

Though the meadowlark has a bright yellow breast, it can hide very well. It keeps its brownish back toward danger, hiding the yellow breast. To protect its nest, the meadowlark carefully walks away from it, then flies up out of the grass at a safe distance.

Father chooses the site

Many meadowlarks leave their northern homes in autumn and fly south, where they live in scattered flocks in South Carolina, Alabama, Louisiana and Texas. Some birds, especially males, do not go south but prefer to remain in sheltered marshes and cut-over hay fields, where they can find food. In spring, these resident birds claim good nesting territories before their rivals come back from the South. Returning females are courted, and during the nesting season a successful male may attract as many as three females to his part of the prairie, but not all at the same nesting time.

Mother is the homemaker

Once she has accepted her mate, the female constructs a well-concealed grassy nest in a hollow in the ground. She builds a dome of growing grass stems over the nest.

Three to seven eggs are laid. The eggs are white with brown and lavender spots and blotches. The female sits on them alone for 13 to 15 days. After the eggs hatch, the male may occasionally help feed the young, but he is most helpful when his mate of the moment goes off to build her second nest. Meadowlarks usually have two families each year.

The meadowlark has habits that make it hard for predators to find its nest. If you see a female carrying grass to a certain spot, it may be a decoy. Several nests may be built before she decides to use one.

After the nest is completed and the eggs are laid, only the female goes there. She never flies directly to the nest. Instead she lands 20 to 50 feet (six to 15 meters) away, then walks to it. When leaving the nest, she uses the same protective measure—she walks away before she flies.

The farmer's friend

Meadowlarks are insect-eating birds that are welcomed by farmers. Cutworms, grasshoppers, beetles and caterpillars are part of the daily menu. In the autumn some weed seeds and waste grain are eaten.

Because meadowlarks build their nests in farm fields and pastures, many nests are lost when clover and alfalfa fields are mowed. Because they are ground nesters, some birds are destroyed by prowling cats, snakes and hawks.

Despite its bright yellow breast, the meadowlark is very hard to see when it is on the ground. By keeping its back toward you, the bird hides its colorful breast and shows only streaked brownish feathers that look much like the surrounding grasses. Except for a tell-tale flicking of its white outer tail feathers when excited, it disappears from sight. You may pass a meadowlark many times without seeing it. And so may its enemy, the hawk.

It is believed that the white outer tail feathers may save many nests from being found by enemies. A predator, in search of a nest with eggs or young, may easily be lured away by an adult bird that lets itself be seen by spreading its tail. When it has led the intruder far from the nest, the adult simply flies away. The nest is safe.

Audubon and the meadowlark

It was not until 1844 that John James Audubon became aware of "curious notes" in the song of meadowlarks he heard in the Missouri River Valley. The bird and the song had been observed by others, including members of the Lewis and Clark expedition, but differences were

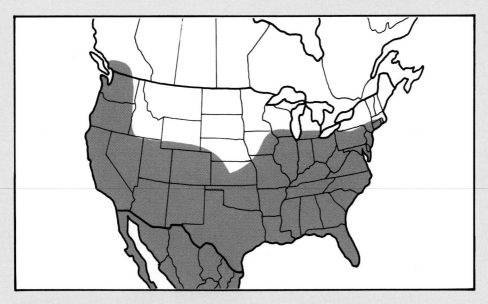

MEADOWLARK FACTS

Habitat: Prairies; open farm fields, meadows, pastures.

Habits: Feed on ground among grasses and herbs where they are well hidden. Males sing from elevated perches.

Food: Cutworms, grasshoppers, beetles, caterpillars, weed seeds and waste grain.

Size: Eastern meadowlark, 9-11 inches (0.23-0.28 meters) long; western meadowlark, 8-10 inches (0.20-0.25 meters) long.

Life Span: Probably three-four years.

Locomotion: When disturbed, it flies from ground with fluttering wings. Conspicuous white patch shows on each side of short, wide tail.

Voice: Eastern meadowlark seems to say "spring o' the year" or "tee-you, tee-year." Western meadowlark has flute-like gurgling melody of 6-10 notes. The two songs are entirely different.

not noted. The sounds heard by Audubon indicated a new species. The eastern meadowlark's scientific name is *Sturnella magna*. *Sturnella* is Latin for "little starling" and *magna* means "large." Audubon added *neglecta*, meaning "neglected or overlooked" to the scientific name *Sturnella* and the new species became *Sturnella neglecta*, the western meadowlark.

The Bison

No animal had a greater influence on the fate of this nation nor symbolized the "Old West" better than the American bison.

Not only is the bison the largest land animal in North America, but it was also the world's most numerous big game animal. There were so many bison in the Great Plains before 1800 that no one could count them. Experts agree they numbered at least 50 million. Some say as many as 125 million bison roamed the prairies at one time.

Spanish explorers could not believe their eyes in 1540 when they saw what is now north Texas black with herds of the big animals. One journalist wrote that they were "like the fish in the sea."

C.H. Townsends, in 1830, reported an eight mile (13 kilometers) wide valley filled rim to rim for 10 miles (16 kilometers) by a single solid mass of buffalo. Luke Voorhees told of riding for 200 miles (320 kilometers) through a series of herds that stretched as far as he could see on horseback. A party on the Arkansas River in Kansas estimated one herd at 25 miles (40 kilometers) wide and 50 miles (80 kilometers) long. They guessed the number of animals at four million. Cavalry General Philip Sheridan and a party of officers rode the 100 miles (160 kilometers) from Fort Dodge to Fort Supply through a solid herd of buffalo estimated at 100 million.

In those days, the bison thrived, for it was well suited to the prairies. It had no significant enemy except humans.

Decline of a great American

How is it possible for the world's most common big game animal nearly to vanish in less than 100 years?

The answer is one of the sorriest chapters in American history. Between the years 1830 and 1900, the bison was slaughtered by humans. The reasons were many, but basically, there was no place in modern America for the great herds of bison. At first, the bison fed and clothed the more than one million pioneers who slowly and painfully made their way across the new land. But with the coming of the railroads, the demand for meat, robes, bones and even sport hunting rose beyond the ability of bison to survive without help.

sin, in the eyes of many settlers, was its value to the Indians. The pioneers knew that every bison killed was one less that could feed, shelter and clothe an Indian family.

Buffalo and native Americans

The bison was the basis of life for the Plains Indians. Its meat was eaten either fresh or dried. Hides were made into robes, moccasins, clothing, tepee coverings, shields, boats and even coffins. The bison's long hair served as jewelry and was braided into rope. Its bladder and stomach made excellent containers for storing food, berries and nuts. The bones were used for bows, tools and toys for children. Ribs were made into sled runners. Horns served as drinking cups, spoons and ladles. Hooves were made into glue. Even the bison's droppings were used as fuel for the Indians' fires.

It is easy to see that as long as bison were plentiful, the Plains Indians prospered. When the animals were destroyed, the Indians suffered severely.

Teams of hunters and skinners moved into the Plains. An expert shot could kill one to three thousand bison a year. It was estimated that between 1850 and 1860, the kill on the northern Plains alone was 2½ million. Of these, 100,000 bison were killed just for their hides. No other use was made of the dead animals.

Perhaps the bison's worst

39

Nature of the beast

There are two kinds of bison in North America: the better known Plains bison and the larger and darker wood bison, which lives in northern Alberta and the Northwest Territories in Canada.

Before whites came, the bison was bothered only by wolves, Indian hunters and the hard-biting flies. Its summers were spent in relative peace and well-fed contentment. To fight the flies, the bison dug great holes in wet spots, where they wallowed, or rolled around in the deep mud. The thick layer of mud dried to a protective coat of armor. Many of the ancient buffalo wallows can still be seen on the Plains.

With the approach of autumn, the great herds of Plains bison moved south, where the winter weather was less severe and the grass more plentiful. When winter broke, they again moved north for the summer.

The leader of the herd was usually an old cow, or female. The bulls, or males, were stationed as guards outside the main herd.

Bison are thriving again, but only in small captive herds. Within these herds, life goes on as before. Cows give birth to one calf in late spring. Twins are

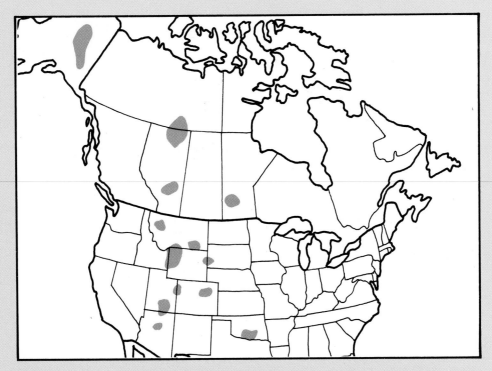

BISON FACTS

Habitat: Plains bison—the American prairie. Wood bison—woodland openings in North.

Habits: Moves slowly in herds, all day long.

Food: A grazer, eats prairie grasses and other plants.

Size and Weight: Average is 1,800 pounds (816 kilograms), but can weigh 2,400 pounds (1,089 kilograms); full-grown bull is six feet (two meters) at the shoulders and 10-12 feet (three-four meters) long, including tail.

Life Span: Fifteen to 20 years, known to have lived 30-40 years.

Locomotion: Usually slow walker, but can run up to 35 miles (55 kilometers) per hour.

Voice: A kind of snort and grunt like a barnyard pig.

rare. When the cow feels that her calf is about to be born, she moves away from the herd to seek a protected area of tall grass. The 30 to 70 pound (15 to 30 kilogram) calf is born with its eyes open. The calf is colored bright yellowish-red, a striking contrast to the deep chocolate brown of the adults. The cow licks it clean. The calf is a bit wobbly as it has its first meal of mother's milk. Bison milk is not plentiful, but it is rich and gives the baby a good start in life.

Within a few days, the calf is strong enough to keep up with the herd. For the first year, it follows its mother. When a new calf is born the following spring, the yearling is on its own as a member of the herd.

The Rattlesnake

The rattlesnake is one of the most dangerous poisonous snakes in the Americas. There are 32 different types of rattlesnakes, and at least one species is found in each of the lower 48 states, except Maine and Delaware.

The prairie rattler is one of the most common. It lives in the Great Plains states east of the Rocky Mountains. The prairie rattler belongs to a group of eight closely related snakes commonly known as western rattlesnakes. The prairie rattlesnake is the most abundant of the eight. Its scientific name is *Crotalus viridis viridis*.

Rattlesnakes are known as pit vipers because they have holes or "pits" on each side of the head between the eye and the nostril. These pits can detect temperature differences in objects. Rattlesnakes use them to locate warm-blooded food at night—chiefly the rodents that are so abundant on the prairie. All rattlesnakes are pit vipers, but not all pit vipers are rattlesnakes. Cottonmouths and copperheads are other examples of pit vipers.

A rattlesnake's rattle scares away animals which may harm it, but—contrary to myth—you can't tell a rattlesnake's age by the number of rattles it has on its tail. A rattlesnake forms a new rattle each time it sheds its skin.

Rattlesnakes are dangerous

Like all rattlesnakes, the prairie rattlesnake kills prey by injecting poison into its body through "fangs" in the snake's mouth. Fangs work like the needles doctors use for giving shots.

The prairie rattlesnake is among the top four snakes that cause human deaths in our country. The copperhead strikes more people, but its bite is seldom fatal. But the wounds are painful from all.

How rattlesnakes rattle

The prairie rattlesnake is named for the rattles it carries at the end of its tail. Each rattle fits loosely into the next, and the rattle or buzzing comes from the pieces hitting against each other when the snake shakes its tail. It probably rattles to scare away animals that might harm the snake. But it doesn't always rattle when it sees a human.

It is not true that you can tell a rattlesnake's age by the number of rattles. A new one is formed each time the snake sheds its skin. When a snake outgrows its old skin, the skin dries and splits at the nose. The snake hooks it on something, such as a branch, and turns it inside out. Off comes the old skin. Underneath is a brand-new and better fitting skin. At the end of one year, a snake may have four of five rattles. A newborn has only one rattle, called a "button."

How fast does a rattlesnake rattle? It all depends. The rattlesnake is cold-blooded. That is, its body temperature depends on the temperature around it. The warmer this cold-blooded

animal gets, the faster it rattles. One with a body temperature of 90 degrees Fahrenheit (32 degrees Celsius) might rattle 100 times a second. Incidentally, 105 degrees Fahrenheit (41 degrees Celsius) is about as hot as a snake can get and still live.

Rattlesnakes are born, not hatched

There are two kinds of snake mothers: Oviparous, those that lay eggs; and viviparous, those whose young leave the mother's body fully developed. The prairie rattlesnake, like all rattlesnakes, is viviparous. When born, the young are 8½ to 11 inches (22 to 28 centimeters) long. There are about 12 babies in each brood. They may grow to be 35 to 45 inches (89 to 114 centimeters) long, not including the rattles. The record length is 57 inches (145 centimeters). Rattlesnake mothers do not take care of their young. Snakes find their own food and are on their own from the time they are born. They have poisonous venom from birth. The bigger they are, the more poison they have.

The prairie rattlesnake is greenish-gray, olive-green or greenish-brown. Its body is marked with dark brown blotches bordered with white. Tail blotches tend to form bands.

Tall snake tales

The prairie rattlesnake is the subject of many myths and tall stories. One of its favorite retreats is an unused prairie dog burrow. Some people think the two animals live together in peace and harmony. The truth is that young prairie dogs and the burrowing owls that also sometimes live in these tunnels make excellent meals for the snakes.

Perhaps you have heard that a cowboy sleeping on the open prairie will coil a rope on the ground around his bed because a rattlesnake will not cross the rope. Nonsense! A snake tries to avoid any object when crawling, but if there is no easy way around it, the snake will crawl over it.

Sometimes people ask, "Does the mate of a dead rattlesnake lie beside the body waiting to seek revenge on the killer?" No! Male and female snakes usually do not stay together after mating.

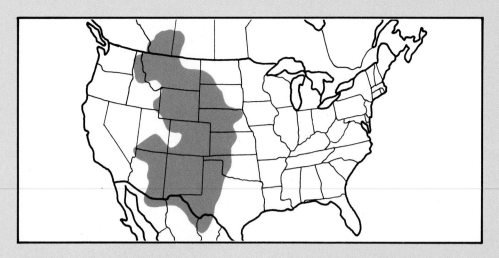

PRAIRIE RATTLESNAKE FACTS

Habitat: Grasslands of the Great Plains; occasionally lower parts of mountains.

Habits: Hibernates in rocky dens in winter. Most active at night and during cooler parts of summer days.

Food: Small mammals and birds, principally. Injects poison into living prey; swallows victims whole.

Size: Thirty-four to 45 inches (89-114 centimeters) long (including rattle). Record length 57 inches (145 centimeters).

Life Span: Perhaps more than 20 years in the wild; one captive rattlesnake lived 28 years, another lived 24 years, 7 months.

Locomotion: On the ground in a series of S-curves, gaining traction from any roughness of the terrain. Average speed less than two miles (three kilometers) per hour.

Voice: Silent except for hissing or rattling.

The Coyote

The lonesome howl of a coyote is one of the great sounds in nature, along with the honking of wild geese and the bugling of a bull elk. But there is much more to this dog-like creature than its chilling call. The coyote belongs to the family of *Canidae*, which includes the wolf, jackal, fox and domestic dog. All members of this group are social creatures. They often hunt in packs and use their running speed to catch food. They have sensitive ears, sharp eyes and a very keen sense of smell. All are intelligent creatures, but the coyote may be the cleverest of all.

A blood brother of the dog, the coyote looks much like a medium-size German shepherd, but is lighter in color. It also acts like a dog in some ways. The coyote's tail wags when it is pleased. When frightened, it holds its tail between its legs. The youngsters play like puppies. When they grow up, coyotes remain playful, despite the hard lives they must lead.

Like a dog, the coyote has a scent gland near the base of its tail. This gland gives each coyote its own individual scent. When coyotes meet, they identify each other by smell.

They also communicate with howls, barks and yaps. Sometimes they howl to signal others that danger is near or that food is available. Some researchers believe they also howl for the fun of it or because they are lonely.

Den full of pups

Coyotes normally range over the open prairie, with no permanent home. But when a female is ready to give birth to a litter of pups in the spring, she will go house hunting for a place to den up. She may prepare as many as 15 dens for safety.

Coyotes are good diggers and will either dig new dens or enlarge the burrows of rabbits, badgers or foxes. Occasionally, they will use rock dens, where no digging is necessary.

The number of pups in a litter depends on the amount of food available. The more food, the greater the number of pups.

Five to seven pups is average, though 19 have been found in a single den.

When the fuzzy, woolly pups are born, they are blind and helpless. During their first few days, the female stays with them while her mate hunts food. By the time the pups are two weeks old, they can see. Within another week, they have their first view of the outside world.

Coyote pups suckle their mother's milk for the first two months, but after about five weeks, they also eat meat brought to them by their parents. The older they get, the more time

they spend outside the den frolicking and tumbling like puppy dogs. Pups are forever hungry at that age and look forward to the arrival of the adults carrying food. They get so anxious that they often go to lookouts where they can watch for their parents' return. Coyotes are very clean animals, and their dens are always tidy and without odor. If a den becomes infested with fleas or other pests, the family moves to another.

As summer turns to autumn, the pups leave the den and learn to hunt. They begin by catching grasshoppers before trying their skills on larger game.

As winter approaches, the family breaks up, though the pups may remain together in twos and threes through the first winter.

War on coyotes

The coyote has a bad reputation among many ranchers of the West. It sometimes kills and eats young calves and sheep. Until recent years, both state and federal government agents helped ranchers destroy coyotes by paying a reward for each one killed. Poison was also used, but it often killed other kinds of wildlife and never really hurt the coyote population.

Some ranchers now protect coyotes because they realize that the animals are helpful. The coyote eats mostly rabbits, prairie dogs and other grass-eating rodents. In other words, coyotes can actually help the rancher by eating the rodents that eat the grass meant for cattle and sheep. But most ranchers still don't see it that way and continue to wage war, without much success, on the craftiest of all the wild dogs.

An adaptable creature

For nearly a century, humans tried every way they could think of to destroy the coyote. We shot, trapped, poisoned and even destroyed the home range of the coyote, but the animal has survived.

Indeed, the coyote's range has spread at a surprising rate, which is further proof that it has learned how to live with humans.

Mainly an animal of the prairies, open plains and desert, the coyote once fed on deer, elk and antelope. But with the westward movement of settlers, the coyote has successfully changed its diet to smaller game such as rodents and rabbits. It has spread as far north as Alaska and south to Costa Rica in Central America.

Only a few decades ago, a report of a coyote in Pennsylvania or New York State was considered impossible. Today, coyotes are rather common in these and other eastern areas. They are now seen from the Deep South to New England.

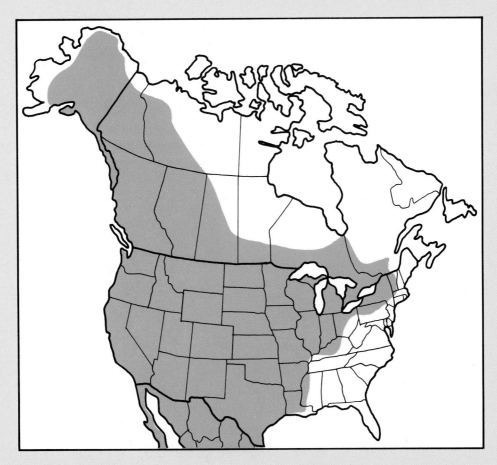

COYOTE FACTS

Habitat: Mostly open plains and desert, but has adapted to nearly all habitats. Dens in ground or rocky areas.

Habits: Most active early morning or late afternoon. Sometimes follows a herd of elk, deer or cattle, which act as "game flushers."

Food: Rabbits, rodents and occasionally sheep and calves. Will also eat dead animals.

Size and Weight: Twenty inches (0.5 meters) high at shoulders, four feet (1.2 meters) long including 11-16 inch (0.28-0.41 meter) tail; 20-25 pounds (9-11 kilograms) average, can get up to 50 pounds (23 kilograms) maximum.

Life Span: Average one-two years; up to 10 in wild; up to 18 in captivity.

Locomotion: Walks and runs like a dog; record 43 miles (69 kilometers) per hour, but seldom runs more than 30 miles (50 kilometers) per hour; 6-10 feet (two-three meters) at each leap.

Voice: Long, mournful, high-pitched howl. Also yips, yaps and barks.

The Prairie Chicken

The greater prairie chicken almost disappeared but now is staging a comeback. Hunters killed large numbers of these birds to sell for meat. This practice was stopped decades ago. Careful management by state governments has saved this delightful bird for us to hear, see and enjoy.

The prairie chicken is best known for the amazing spring performance it gives on its "booming grounds." On the wide open prairie, males, or cocks, gather year after year to dance and boom. The purpose is to attract females, or hens, at mating time.

Picture this performance: A cock bird starts to stomp his feet rapidly on the ground. As he dances up and down, orange-shaped and orange-colored air sacs on the sides of his neck fill up with air like small balloons. Wings are dropped to the ground. The cock fans his tail. Pointed neck feathers are raised. Orange eyebrows puff out. The male prairie chicken is ready to "boom." He makes a hollow sound and lets out the air in his orange neck sacs. You can make a similar sound by blowing over the top of an empty bottle.

Another male nearby, seeing and hearing this display, answers with one of his own. Another and still another take up the challenge. All go through the same performance. Soon dancing and booming are everywhere.

To see and hear this great show you must hide nearby at dawn, the best time for booming. When the sun comes up, the males disappear in the tall prairie grass, and the show is over until evening.

Range and family

The prairie chicken lives in the Dakotas east to Wisconsin and south to Colorado, Oklahoma, Missouri and Illinois. However, numbers are small. One race, Attwater's prairie chicken, which survives only in 10 Texas counties, is endangered. There are only about 1,500 birds of this race left.

Another race, the lesser prairie chicken, lives in the grassy prairies of Colorado, Kansas, Oklahoma, New Mexico and Texas. It is less common than the greater prairie chicken.

The prairie chicken is a member of the grouse family. Living with it on the prairies is a close relative, the sharp-tailed grouse. This bird has a pointed white tail, while the prairie chicken's tail is short, rounded and dark.

One relative of the prairie chicken is gone forever—the heath hen. It lived along the Atlantic seacoast in the northeastern part of our country. Colonists enjoyed many heath hen dinners, but too much hunting and loss of its homeland to farming killed off the bird. The last heath hen was seen in 1931.

Life on the prairie

Hen prairie chickens for miles around are attracted to the booming grounds of the males. It is time for them to nest and raise a family.

After mating, the hen seeks a well-hidden place in tall grass. There she hollows out a nest for her dozen or so brown-spotted, olive-colored eggs.

In 23 or 24 days the eggs hatch, and the female leads her brood onto the surrounding prairie in search of bugs, berries, seeds and grain. The male prairie chicken leaves all these duties to the hen. When his booming and dancing days are done, his work and responsibilities are over for the year.

That the prairie chicken may live

The prairie chicken will, it is hoped, escape the sad fate of the heath hen. Our government and conservationists are working together to preserve the prairie chicken. Several states are buying lands where these birds can live undisturbed by people.

In Wisconsin a special arrangement provides that local governments will not lose tax money when lands are set aside. The Department of Natural Resources and several private groups have joined forces to buy 11,000 acres (28,500 square kilometers) of land and maintain it. In this way, the best range for prairie chickens has been preserved.

The federal government has come to the rescue of the Attwater's prairie chicken by buying land for a national wildlife refuge. In Texas, 10,000 acres (25,900 square kilometers) have been set aside so that this race will continue to exist. If we are fortunate, there may be even more of these interesting birds in the future.

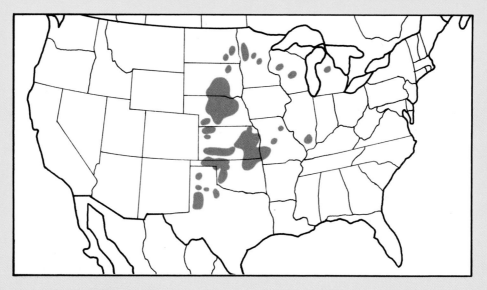

PRAIRIE CHICKEN FACTS

Habitat: Prairies and brushy grasslands.

Habits: In spring, males dance together on "booming" grounds where they gather at sunrise and sundown to attract females. Males and females do not pair, so females nest and care for young alone. They do not migrate.

Food: Tender leaves of herbs and grasses; seeds, sedges, insects, berries.

Size: Greater and Attwater's prairie chickens, 16-18 inches (41-46 centimeters) long; lesser prairie chickens, 15-16 inches (38-41 centimeters).

Locomotion: Spends most time on ground. Flight direct and fast punctuated by gliding. Can outfly a peregrine falcon in straight and level flight.

Life Span: Up to seven years; average about four years if they survive the first year.

Voice: Cackles and clucks much like a chicken. On spring "booming" grounds, males inflate air sacs and make a drawnout cooing sound, "oo-loo-woo," something between organ music and blowing across the opening of a bottle. Never loud, even when close, but can be heard up to four miles (six kilometers).

What Can YOU Do?

Before the white man arrived in North America, the prairie grasslands covered the center of the continent, from northern Canada to the Gulf of Mexico and from the Appalachians to the Rockies. Today, the prairies, like the buffalo and prairie dogs that lived on it, are nearly gone. We have converted the prairies into farmland for crops and grazing land for cattle. We have built roads across it and strung wire around and through it. Today, most of the remaining true prairies are found in preserves where they are protected.

What is the solution?

1. Prairies are being preserved and restored in parks and conservation areas. Some are being managed by states, others by agencies of the federal government. Write to the following agencies for more information on prairies: Missouri Prairie Foundation, Box 200, Columbia, MO 65201; Tallgrass Prairie Foundation, 5450 Buena Vista, Shawnee Mission, KS 66205; the conservation departments of any of the prairie states; the Great Lakes Chapter, Sierra Club, 616 Dalles Road, Wheaton, IL 60187; Northern Environmental Council, Christie Building, Duluth, MN 55802.

2. The federal government is considering preservation of additional prairie lands. Write to your Congressman to tell him you would like to see more of the prairie preserved for the years ahead. Ask him for information about proposals now being discussed.

3. The coyote and the rattlesnake are being relentlessly hunted and killed in large numbers in many states. Join a group that works for wildlife. Groups of people often can accomplish more than one person working alone. They have been effective in protecting prairie wildlife. Conservation groups saved the buffalo and the prairie chicken. Numbers now are increasing.

Projects you can do

Visit a prairie
If you live close to a prairie park or preserved prairie area, visit it. You will see how the central area of North America appeared 200 years ago.

Plant a prairie
Find out from the library or the county agricultural agent what kinds of plants grow on the prairies. Either plant the prairie in your school yard, or indoors in a box of soil. Write prairie organizations listed at right for seed information.

Collect prairie paintings
There were a number of famous artists who painted scenes from the prairies when the pioneers were crossing them. Some of these paintings show how the Plains Indians lived. Make a collection of prairie paintings from books and magazines that tell the story of the prairies in art.

Why Indians needed the buffalo
List all the things that the buffalo provided for the Plains Indians. Have the class bring to school samples of these items, which come from other sources today. Let each class member talk about one way the buffalo helped the Indians survive on the prairie.

Visit prairie animals
The prairie animals listed in this book are frequently found in a zoo. How many are in your nearby zoo? If you have a camera, take pictures of them the next time you visit. Look for the meadowlark in open fields and pastures. Record its song. The meadowlark is one of the most numerous birds in America.

While you're in a prairie...

There are many things each of us can do to protect the prairie and its wildlife. Know what to do and not to do on a prairie.

Be careful with fires
In the fall and winter, prairie grass is very dry. It burns easily and a fire is difficult to control out in the windy open spaces. In pioneer times prairie fires burned over hundreds of square miles. Be very careful in building a fire in grass country.

Stay on trails
Most prairie parks have marked trails. Stay on them and don't take shortcuts. A path soon kills fragile plants and can lead to erosion. In some prairie areas tracks made by wagons of the pioneers 100 years ago still are visible.

Don't be a litterbug
Don't leave garbage and other trash in prairie grass. Keep the prairie fresh and clean as it was before the white man moved west.

Protect wintering wildlife
Do not disturb animals during the winter. Winter is a time of stress for prairie wildlife. Grass frequently is buried under deep snow. High winds and drifting snow make prairie country dangerous for both man and animals.

Leave baby wildlife alone
If you come across a baby animal, leave it alone. Chances are the mother is hiding nearby. Besides, there's little chance that the creature will survive if you attempt to care for it at home. In most states, it's illegal to capture infant animals.

TEXT AND DESIGN: Market Communications, Inc.
Cliff Ganschow, chairman
H. Lee Schwanz, president
Glenn Helgeland, editorial director
Al Jacobs, art director
George Harrison, senior editor
Hal H. Harrison, Kit Harrison
and Valjean McLenighan, associate editors
Cheryl S. Bernard, Cynthia Swanson, Kathy
Sieja, Nanci Krajcir and Nancy Branson,
editorial assistants
Faith Williams, Robin Berens and Maureen Maguire,
production staff

PHOTOGRAPHERS: Ralph H. Williams (Bruce Coleman, Inc.):
   Front Cover
Grant Heilman: Title Page, Back Cover: Pages 18, 22, 36, 38-39
Wayne Lankinen (Bruce Coleman, Inc.): Page 19
H. Engels (Bruce Coleman, Inc.): Pages 20-21
L. R. Ditto (Bruce Coleman, Inc.): Page 17
Charles G. Summers, Jr. (Bruce Coleman, Inc.): Pages 43, 45, 59
Joe Branney (Bruce Coleman, Inc.): Page 44
Alan Blank (Bruce Coleman, Inc.): Page 46
Leonard Lee Rue III: Pages 40, 56
Leonard Lee Rue III (Bruce Coleman, Inc.): Page 34
Gary R. Zahm (Bruce Coleman, Inc.): Page 58
Hal H. Harrison: Pages 32, 60
Nicholas deVore III (Bruce Coleman, Inc.): Page 54
Wolfgang Bayer (Bruce Coleman, Inc.): Pages 49, 50
Jen & Des Bartlett (Bruce Coleman, Inc.): Pages 52-53
Wardene Weisser (Bruce Coleman, Inc.): Page 33
George Harrison: Page 30
Joe Van Wormer (Bruce Coleman, Inc.): Pages 10, 12, 14, 27
J. Couffer (Bruce Coleman, Inc.): Page 13
Lynn M. Stone (Bruce Coleman, Inc.): Page 9
M. P. L. Fogden (Bruce Coleman, Inc.): Pages 24, 26
Jeff Foott (Bruce Coleman, Inc.): Page 28
J. R. Simon (Bruce Coleman, Inc.): Page 27

ART: Jay Blair: Pages 6-7